Welcome to "The Timeless Colours of Palestine," a
that goes beyond mere art—it's a journey into the h.... .. . .
and its people.

Palestine, with its rolling olive groves, ancient streets, and vibrant
culture, stands as a testament to the resilience of the human spirit.
For generations, Palestinians have faced the challenges of
displacement, conflict, and the struggle for recognition, yet their
hope and determination remain unshaken.

This book seeks to do more than just tell a story. It aims to connect
you, through every stroke of color, to the dreams and aspirations of
a people yearning for freedom and sovereignty. Each page you turn
and color is a step into the world of Palestinians—a world where
despite the hardships, the culture thrives and the spirit endures.

As you embark on this coloring journey, remember that each image
is a representation of life in Palestine—the joys, the sorrows, the
unyielding hope. From the ancient city of Jerusalem to the serene
landscapes of the countryside, you are not just witnessing a place,
but you are engaging with a narrative of resilience and aspiration.

Through your colors, you become part of this narrative. You are not
just an observer but an active participant in the commemoration and
celebration of Palestinian heritage and their undying dream for a
future where they can live in peace, dignity, and freedom.

We hope that "The Timeless Colours of Palestine" offers you both
an artistic escape and a meaningful reflection on the enduring
strength of the Palestinian people. May this book be a window to
understanding, a bridge of solidarity, and a canvas for your
imagination.

- Omar Uddin

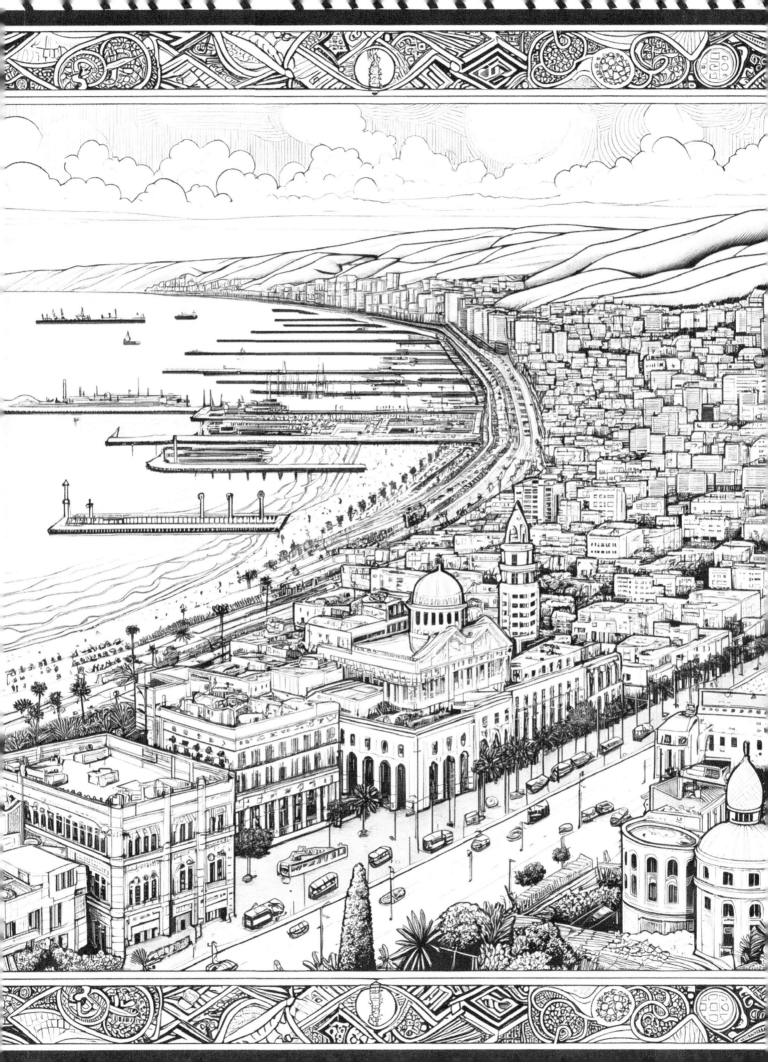

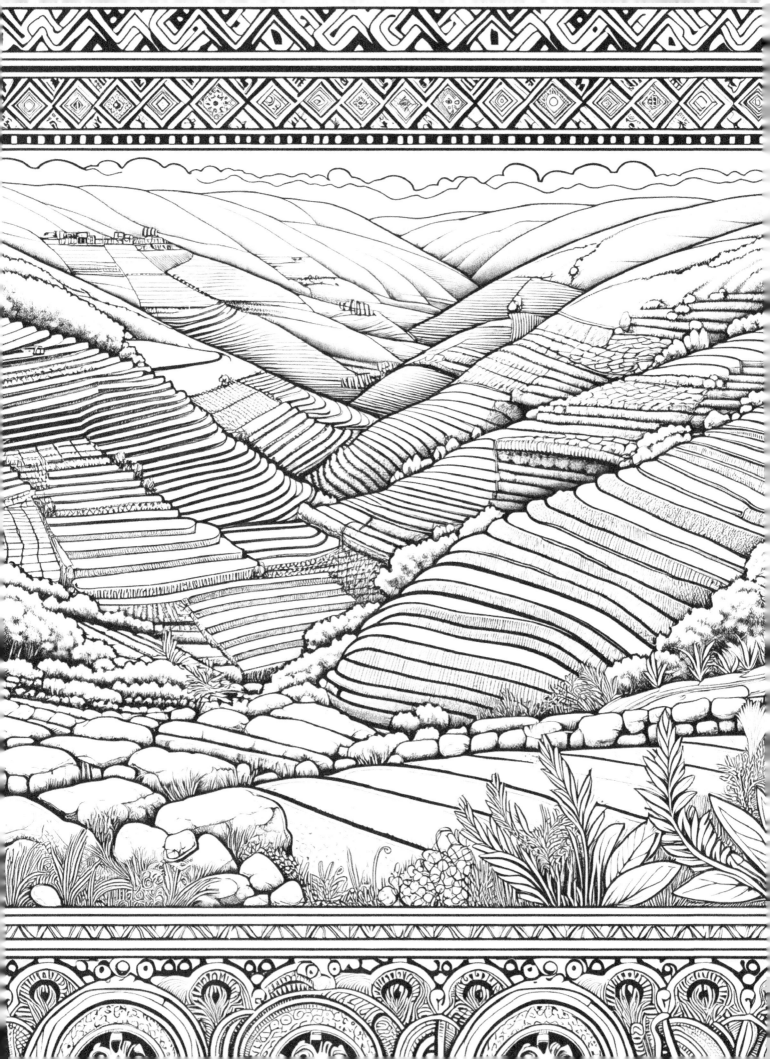

Printed in Great Britain
by Amazon